Isaac Asimov's
21st Century
Library of the Universe

Near and Far

Our Planetary System

BY ISAAC ASIMOV
WITH REVISIONS AND UPDATING BY RICHARD HANTULA

Gareth Stevens Publishing
A WORLD ALMANAC EDUCATION GROUP COMPANY

Please visit our web site at: www.garethstevens.com
For a free color catalog describing Gareth Stevens Publishing's list of high-quality
books and multimedia programs, call 1-800-542-2595 (USA) or 1-800-387-3178 (Canada).
Gareth Stevens Publishing's fax: (414) 332-3567.

Library of Congress Cataloging-in-Publication Data

Asimov, Isaac.
    Our planetary system / by Isaac Asimov; with revisions and updating by Richard Hantula.
      p. cm. — (Isaac Asimov's 21st century library of the universe. Near and far)
    Includes bibliographical references and index.
    ISBN 0-8368-3969-2 (lib. bdg.)
    1. Solar system—Juvenile literature. I. Hantula, Richard. II. Title.
    QB501.3.A855   2005
    523.2—dc22   2004058466

This edition first published in 2005 by
Gareth Stevens Publishing
A WRC Media Company
330 West Olive Street, Suite 100
Milwaukee, WI 53212 USA

Series editor: Mark J. Sachner
Cover design and layout adaptation: Melissa Valuch
Picture research: Kathy Keller
Additional picture research: Diane Laska-Swanke
Artwork commissioning: Kathy Keller and Laurie Shock
Production director: Jessica Morris

The editors at Gareth Stevens Publishing have selected science author Richard Hantula to bring
this classic series of young people's information books up to date. Richard Hantula has written
and edited books and articles on science and technology for more than two decades. He was
the senior U.S. editor for the *Macmillan Encyclopedia of Science.*

In addition to Hantula's contribution to this most recent edition, the editors would like to
acknowledge the participation of two noted science authors, Greg Walz-Chojnacki and
Francis Reddy, as contributors to earlier editions of this work.

Contents

• Our Planetary System •

We live in an enormously large place – the Universe. It's only natural that we would want to understand this place, so scientists and engineers have developed instruments and spacecraft that have told us far more about the Universe than we could possibly imagine.

We have seen planets up close, and spacecraft have even landed on some. We have learned about quasars and pulsars, supernovas and colliding galaxies, and black holes and dark matter. We have gathered amazing data about how the Universe may have come into being and how it may end. Nothing could be more astonishing.

The planets we have seen up close, so far, are all members of the Sun's family. They are worlds that orbit the Sun, as Earth itself does. A large number of smaller bodies also belong to the Sun's family, which we call the Solar System. *Sol* is the Latin word for "Sun," and the Sun is the central and largest object of the system. All the components of our Solar System are quite different from one another, and each is, in its own way, a fascinating place.

A nebula ripe for star formation. Stars have already begun to form out of the vast cloud.

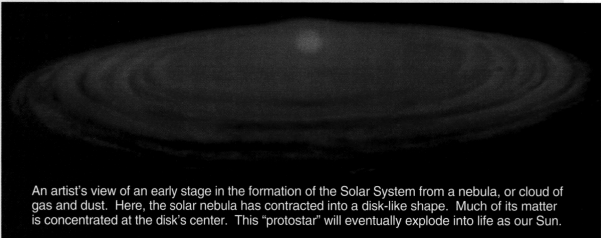

An artist's view of an early stage in the formation of the Solar System from a nebula, or cloud of gas and dust. Here, the solar nebula has contracted into a disk-like shape. Much of its matter is concentrated at the disk's center. This "protostar" will eventually explode into life as our Sun.

Nebulous Beginnings

Our Solar System — the Sun together with the planets and other bodies that revolve around it — has not always existed.

Most astronomers say that the Solar System began to develop close to 5 billion years ago. At that time there were no planets, no moons, and no Sun. Instead, scientists think, there was a huge cloud of dust and gas called a nebula.

This nebula was slowly turning, or rotating. It was held together by its own gravity, which caused it to slowly contract. As it grew smaller, the nebula gradually became flatter — coming to look something like a disk — and swirled faster and faster.

Above: The spectacular Eagle Nebula is an important star formation site. It is made up of both brightly glowing gas clouds and darker clouds of dust and gas that show up as black spots in this photograph.

5

A Star Is Born — Our Sun

Let's look more closely at "our" nebula, the cloud we think started our Solar System. Hydrogen and helium made up more than 99 percent of the nebula. They are the two simplest elements and were formed at the beginning of the Universe. Heavier elements made up the rest of the nebula — less than 1 percent. They had formed during the lives and explosive deaths of stars that were much larger than our Sun. These explosions spread the heavier elements throughout space.

As the solar nebula shrank, most of the material fell to its center and gathered into a huge ball of gas. At the center of this ball, matter became very hot and tightly packed. In this heat and pressure, hydrogen atoms collided and combined with each other to form helium.

This process is called nuclear fusion. The fusion released huge amounts of energy. As this energy spread to the outer layers of the ball, it began to glow. A star — our Sun — was born!

Our Solar System: a cosmic pizza with everything — to go!

All the planets move around the Sun in the same direction. They all have orbits that are similar to circles. They all move in almost the same plane. That is, if you built a model of the Solar System with all the planetary orbits represented by curved wires, you could fit the whole thing into the kind of box that pizzas come in. When scientists were investigating how our Solar System began, they wondered how the planets got to be so evenly spread out. This pizza-like shape helped lead them to the idea of a contracting and rapidly swirling cloud of dust and gas.

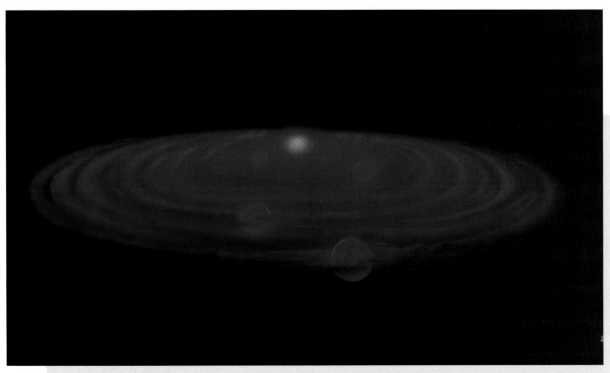

Above: The solar nebula, with the glowing young Sun at its center, continues to contract. The young planets are clearly visible within the swirling disk.

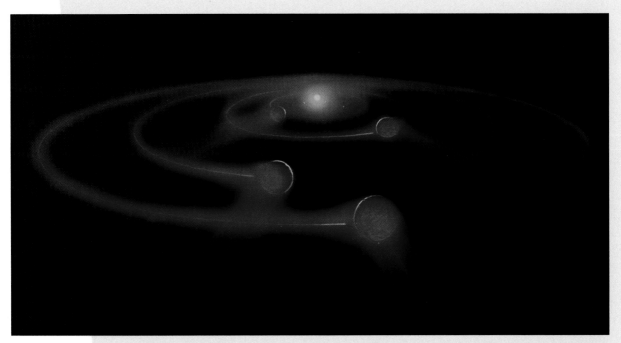

Above: This diagram shows the paths of the early inner planets – Mercury, Venus, Earth, and Mars – as they continue to capture material and grow.

The Planets — Particles in Collision

Away from the center of the cloud, the dust and gas were thinner, and they collected into a "protoplanetary disk."

Tiny particles began to form in the disk. Nearer the center, where it was hotter, only rocky elements could become solid particles, since icy material would be vaporized. Farther from the Sun, icy material could also form particles. All these particles began to collide and stick together, forming larger clumps. Some clumps grew more quickly than others, and their increased mass gave them greater gravity. This allowed them to gather more material and grow even more quickly. Rocky planets formed where the temperatures were high nearer the Sun. The planets known as gas giants formed farther away from the heat of the Sun.

Below and opposite: An artist's conception of how our Solar System began.

Above: Youthful planets, called protoplanets, and moons formed out of the protoplanetary disk that encircled the early Sun.

Above: A great wind of energy from the young Sun blew away much of the remaining nebular matter. Left behind were mainly solid particles – and the Sun – that make up our Solar System as we know it today.

Above: The completed Solar System as seen from beyond the planet Jupiter.

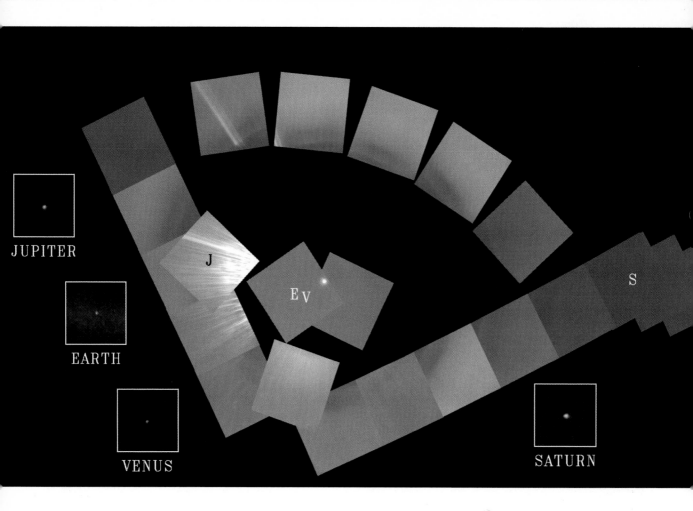

JUPITER

EARTH

VENUS

SATURN

J

E V

S

The Sun: Ruler of Our Solar System

The Sun is, by far, the largest member of our Solar System. It weighs about five hundred times as much as everything else in our Solar System put together! It is the only object in our Solar System large enough for its center to undergo nuclear fusion. Therefore, it is able to produce so much energy that it shines.

Even the biggest planet – Jupiter – is much smaller than the Sun.

Because the planets are so small, nuclear fusion cannot occur at their centers. Their centers may be warm, but their surfaces are relatively cold. They shine only by reflecting light from the Sun.

In addition to the planets, there are many smaller bodies in our Solar System. Most of them circle the Sun as the planets do, but a few circle the planets themselves as natural satellites, or moons.

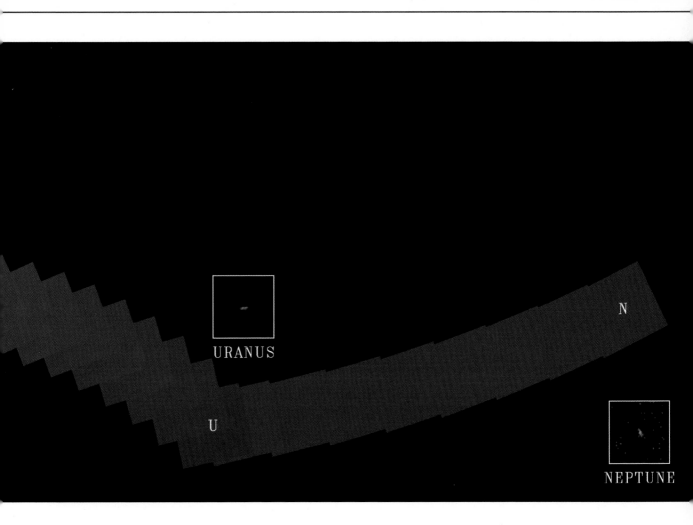

URANUS

U

N

NEPTUNE

Above and opposite: A "portrait" of much of our Solar System, taken in 1990 by the space probe *Voyager 1* from beyond the orbit of the planet Pluto. This picture gives an idea of how tiny the planets look when seen from far away. In the insets, the planets are shown magnified many times. The bright Sun had to be blocked out of this portrait in order for the planets to be easily seen.

A companion star? Why not?

Most stars have at least one companion star. Pairs of stars that orbit around each other are called binary stars. The star nearest to us (other than our Sun), Proxima Centauri, is part of a triple-star system. But as far as we know, our Sun is a single star. There is no other bright star near it. Could there be a tiny star companion of our Sun? Some astronomers have suggested that there might be a dim star near our Sun, and we just haven't noticed it yet!

A cutaway view of Mars showing the structure of a typical rocky planet. The diagram is not to scale. The thickness of the crust is similar to the skin of an apple compared to the rest of the apple. It is quite thin.

The Rocky Planets

The planets that formed quite near the Sun grew very warm because of the Sun's tremendous heat. Hot gases, especially if they are light, are harder to hold by gravitational pull than cold gases. The planets nearest the Sun could not hold the very light hydrogen and helium that made up most of the swirling material. They could only hold onto the small amount of matter that made up its heavier gases, metal, and rock. The planets nearest the Sun are, therefore, much smaller than most of the planets that formed farther away from the Sun. These nearby planets – Mercury, Venus, Earth, and Mars – are mostly rock with metal at the center. They are sometimes called the rocky planets.

Left: The rocky planets are actually quite small compared to the giant planets that formed farther away from the Sun. *Left, top and bottom,* are Earth and Venus. Just to the right of Earth are Mars, Mercury, and Earth's Moon. Immediately below are Io and Europa (both moons of Jupiter). Below them are Ganymede and Callisto, also moons of Jupiter. Below them is Titan, Saturn's largest moon.

The Gas Giants

The planets that formed farther from the Sun were cooler than the nearer planets. At such a great distance, the hydrogen and helium in the protoplanetary disk were cold enough for the planets to hold them with gravitation. That meant these planets grew still larger and had even stronger gravitational pulls that could attract still more gas. The outer planets, except for tiny Pluto (which some scientists do not even consider a planet), grew much larger than the inner ones. Instead of being mainly rock and metal, they are made up mostly of the two gases hydrogen and helium. For that reason, and because they are so large, Jupiter, Saturn, Uranus, and Neptune are called the gas giants.

Right: A cutaway of the gas giant Uranus. The planet's core is made of rock. Above the core is a "sea" made mostly of water, ammonia, and methane. Above that is a gaseous atmosphere made mostly of hydrogen.

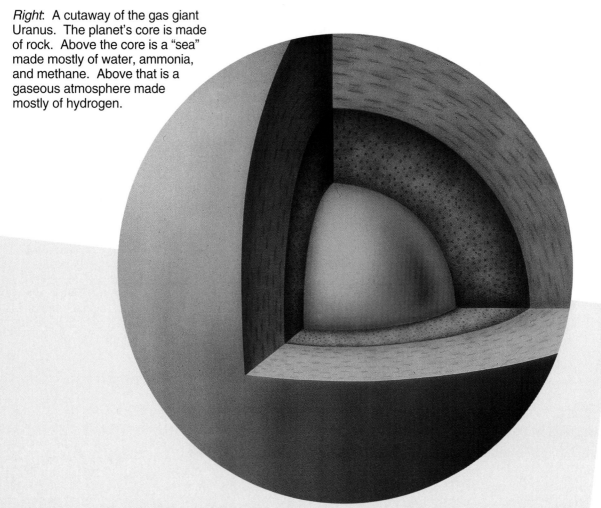

Above: The gas giant Saturn, with its beautiful rings, as photographed by the spacecraft *Cassini* in May 2004.

Right: The gas giant Jupiter.

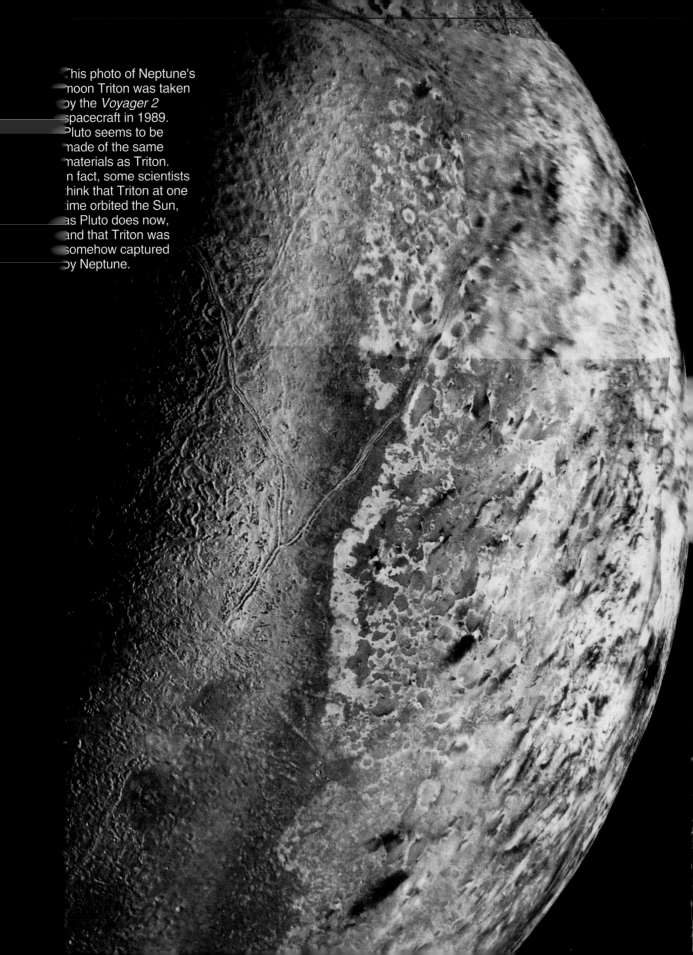

This photo of Neptune's moon Triton was taken by the *Voyager 2* spacecraft in 1989. Pluto seems to be made of the same materials as Triton. In fact, some scientists think that Triton at one time orbited the Sun, as Pluto does now, and that Triton was somehow captured by Neptune.

Pluto's Lopsided Orbit

Remote Pluto is not a gas giant and in fact is even smaller than the inner planets. It is made up of a mixture of rock and ice. It is the biggest of the known bodies that lie in the region of the Solar System called the Kuiper Belt, which stretches far beyond the orbit of Neptune. Pluto itself has a very lopsided orbit, and at one end it even comes in a little closer to the Sun than does Neptune. Pluto's orbit is tilted, though, and there is no chance of a collision with Neptune.

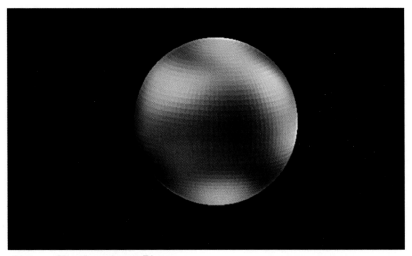

Above: The tiny planet Pluto.

Pluto – the missing planet?

Pluto was discovered during a search for a "missing planet." Astronomers watched the motions of Uranus and Neptune and thought their movements were being affected by the gravity of another distant planet. When Pluto was discovered, many scientists thought they had found what was affecting the motions of Uranus and Neptune. But Pluto is much too small to influence the motions of these planets. Astronomers now believe that the motions of Uranus and Neptune simply had not been measured accurately, and there was no missing planet.

Circling Satellites

As the planets formed, some material in the protoplanetary disk remained separate. These particles eventually joined together to create small bodies, some of which became natural satellites, or moons, of planets. All the gas giants have moons orbiting them. Jupiter, the biggest planet, has four large satellites and dozens of smaller ones. Saturn has one large satellite and numerous middle-sized and small moons. Uranus has a number of middle-sized and small satellites, and Neptune has one large and several small moons. Little Pluto has a single satellite. Of the rocky planets, only Mars and the Earth have satellites. Mars has two tiny ones, but Earth's Moon is quite large. Many scientists believe the Moon was formed from material thrown off when the Earth was struck by a large body.

Above: Photos of six of our Solar System's largest natural satellites, compared in size. Our Moon *(center)* is surrounded by *(clockwise from lower right)* Saturn's Titan plus Jupiter's Callisto, Io, Europa, and Ganymede.

Above: Mars's moons, Phobos *(right)* and Deimos *(left),* do not look much like Earth's Moon. Rather than being round, they are oddly shaped and look like asteroids. In fact, astronomers suspect these moons were once asteroids that were captured by Mars's gravity.

Right: A close-up picture of Saturn's small satellite Phoebe, made by the spacecraft *Cassini* in mid-2004.

This photograph shows our first close look at an asteroid. The spacecraft *Galileo* took this picture of Gaspra in 1991. Gaspra is about 12 miles (19 kilometers) long.

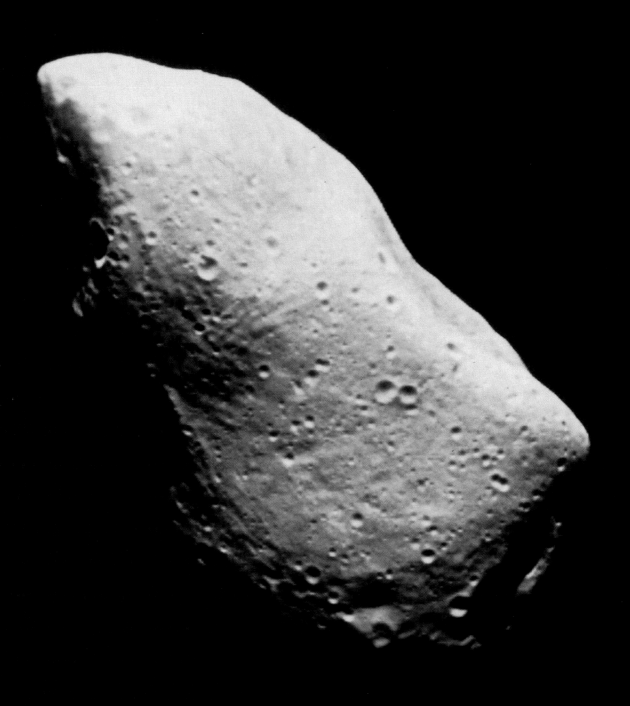

The Asteroid Belt – Cosmic Rubble

The first asteroid, or "minor planet," to be discovered was Ceres in 1801. Since that time, astronomers have known there is more to our Solar System than the moons and planets.

Most asteroids orbit the Sun in a belt between Mars and Jupiter. Some are as large as a few hundred miles (km) across, but most are much smaller. Scientists estimate, however, that more than 1 million

asteroids in the belt are at least 3/5 mile (1 km) wide.

A small number of asteroids follow orbits that take them closer to the Sun than Mars or even the Earth. Two groups of asteroids known as the Trojans precede and follow Jupiter in its orbit around the Sun.

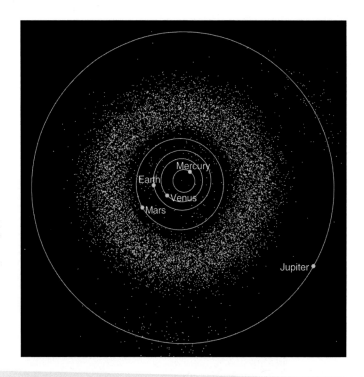

Right: This diagram shows the locations of the known asteroids on January 1, 1995. You can see that most lie between the orbits of Jupiter and Mars. The Trojan asteroids lie near Jupiter's orbit, ahead of and behind the planet.

Planning a trip to another sun?

Before you do, you should have some numbers handy! The planets are spread out over great distances. Earth is about 93 million miles (150 million km) from the Sun, but the outer planets are much farther away. The average distance of Pluto from the Sun is about 3.7 billion miles (5.9 billion km) – 40 times greater than the Earth's distance from the Sun. There is, however, plenty of room for our Solar System to spread out. Beyond it, there are no other stars for trillions of miles (km). The very nearest star, Proxima Centauri, is nearly 7,000 times as far away from us as Pluto – about 25 trillion miles (40 trillion km)!

21

Target: Earth

In 1932, astronomers discovered an asteroid that did not orbit in the belt between Mars and Jupiter. Instead, it passed near our own planet. Then scientists began finding more and more objects that wandered well beyond the asteroid belt.

By 2004, hundreds of asteroids had been discovered that crossed or came close to Earth's orbit and were at least 3/5 mile (1 km) wide. The biggest was about 25 miles (40 km) across. None of the known "near-Earth asteroids" in this range of sizes were expected to collide with our planet in the foreseeable future.

Tiny objects strike Earth's atmosphere all the time. "Shooting stars," or meteors, are nothing more than space rocks burning up in the atmosphere. But somewhat larger objects also strike our atmosphere from time to time, some creating blasts as large as nuclear explosions. Fortunately, these explosions usually occur high above Earth's surface, where they do no harm.

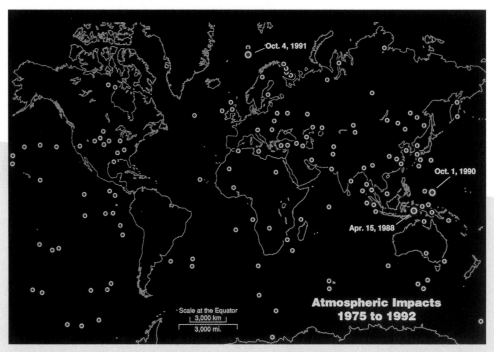

Above: This map shows the locations of 136 asteroid explosions detected by spy satellites between 1975 and 1992. Scientists think the amount represents only a small portion of all the actual blasts.

Above: Many small unseen space rocks lurk near Earth. Perhaps a few times a month, one heads for Earth and explodes high above the surface.

Above: Lively "shooting stars" can perk up a night of stargazing. These are meteors, tiny visitors from space that streak briefly through the sky and bum up in our atmosphere.

23

Billions of Bodies

There are probably thousands of icy bodies in the Kuiper Belt, which begins at about the orbit of Neptune and extends out to somewhere beyond the orbit of Pluto. Pluto is the biggest object found in this belt so far, but a few other bodies have been seen that are larger than Ceres, the biggest asteroid. In 2003, astronomers discovered Sedna, a body that orbits the Sun in a lopsided orbit lying beyond the Kuiper Belt. It seems to be not much smaller than Pluto.

Scientists believe that beyond Sedna there is a region called the Oort Cloud. This cloud surrounds the parts of the Solar System that lie closer to the Sun. It consists of billions of icy comets. Every once in a while something happens that causes one of these small objects to drop toward the Sun. When the object enters the inner region of the Solar System, the Sun's heat vaporizes some of its ice, freeing gas and dust to form the bright head and tail for which comets are famous. The Kuiper Belt is also a source of comets. Some comets travel around the Sun in orbits that do not take them as far out as the Kuiper Belt.

An artist's idea of what the remote body called Sedna might look like.

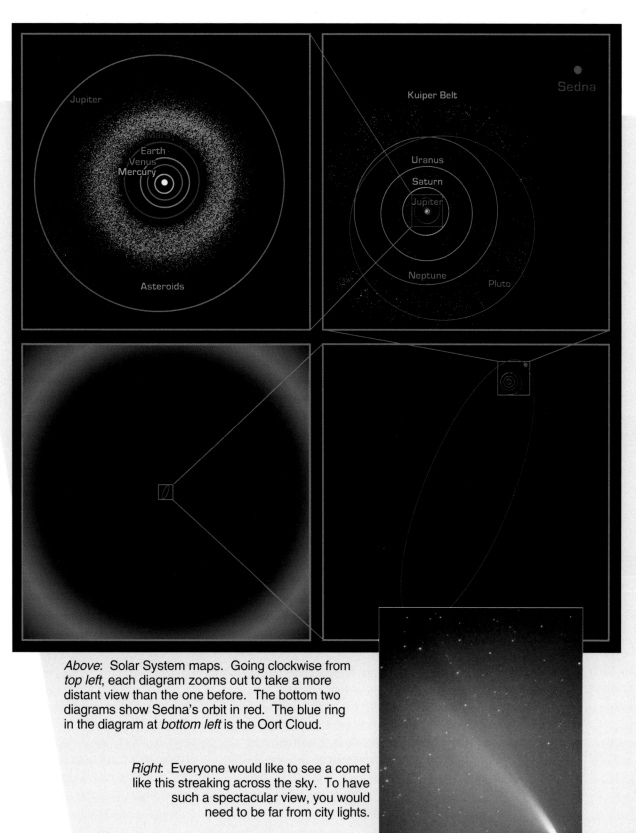

Above: Solar System maps. Going clockwise from *top left*, each diagram zooms out to take a more distant view than the one before. The bottom two diagrams show Sedna's orbit in red. The blue ring in the diagram at *bottom left* is the Oort Cloud.

Right: Everyone would like to see a comet like this streaking across the sky. To have such a spectacular view, you would need to be far from city lights.

Planets Galore

Toward the end of the twentieth century, astronomers began finding evidence that our Sun is not the only star with planets. Close-up images of some stars revealed disk-like shapes that looked like protoplanetary disks. Using advanced techniques, scientists detected individual planets around some stars. By 2004, astronomers had found well over 100 planets of various kinds, with more being discovered all the time.

No one knows how many stars have planets. But since there may be as many as 400 billion stars in our Galaxy, and since there are more than 100 billion other galaxies, it does not seem impossible that somewhere there might even be an Earthlike planet that supports life as we know it!

Below: A false-color picture of the edge of a disk around the star known as Beta Pictoris. Beta Pictoris itself has been blocked out so that its bright light would not interfere with seeing the disk. The discovery of the disk in the 1980s was one of the first bits of strong evidence that our Sun might not be the only star to have a planetary system.

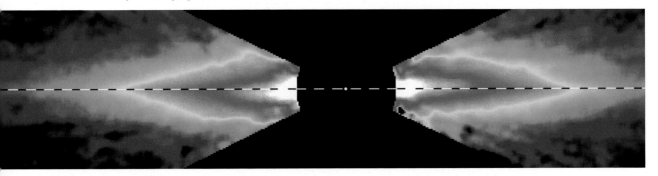

Clouds of comets – stepping stones to the stars?

Astronomers have never seen the Oort Cloud, the collection of comets that is supposed to lie far beyond the planets. But there are reasons to think it exists. If it does exist, no one knows how far out it stretches. It is possible the cloud extends outward for a considerable part of the distance to the nearest star, Proxima Centauri. Does Proxima Centauri also have a cloud of comets reaching out toward Earth? It is interesting to imagine comets all the way across between Earth and Proxima Centauri, like a bridge between us and our nearest stellar neighbor.

Right: An artist's conception of a young star circled by full-sized planets and rings of planetary dust. The rings, known as "debris discs," are formed when young planets collide with one another and smash to pieces, leaving only dust trails in their place.

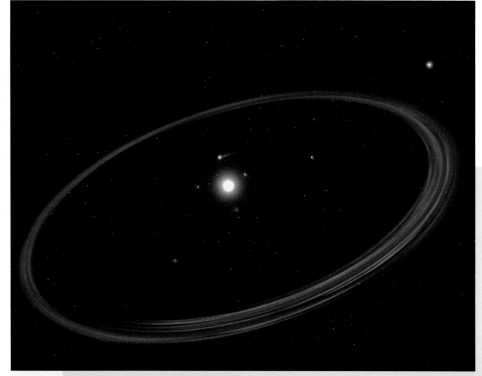

Below: An artist's idea of how the formation of planets in a young solar system might look.

Fact File: Our Home – The Milky Way

Our Solar System began in roughly the same remote corner of the Milky Way Galaxy in which we live today. Nearly 5 billion years ago, our Sun took shape out of a swirling cloud of gas and dust called a nebula. A few "short" million years later, the planets evolved out of the swirling solar nebula.

A view from our perch on the inner edge of the Milky Way. The swirling galactic center glows thousands of light-years away.

The Life of Our Sun

The Sun formed from the first contractions of gas and dust into a solar nebula nearly 5 billion years ago. In the end, many billions of years after its birth, scientists expect its final form to be that of a cold black dwarf. The Sun as we know it is called a main-sequence star. This part of its life, expected to last a total of about 12 billion years, began when nuclear fusion started taking place in the Sun. The beginning of the end will be when the Sun becomes a red giant - perhaps 7 billion years from now. The chart on the next page shows the estimated age of the Sun at key stages in its life. Note that the ages are given in millions of years. For example, the Sun's present age is said to be 4,600 million years - which is the same as 4.6 billion years.

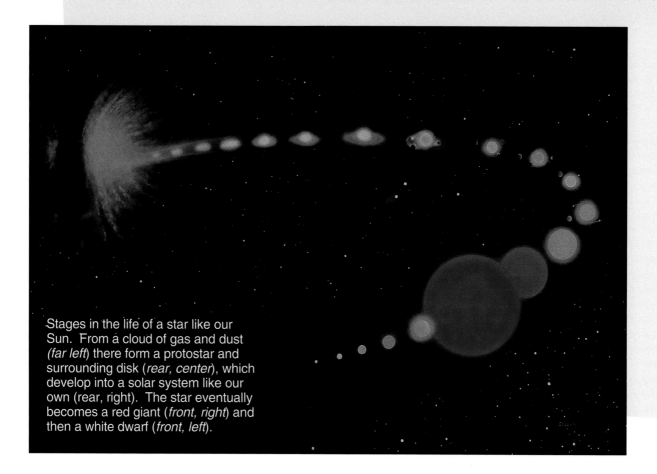

Stages in the life of a star like our Sun. From a cloud of gas and dust *(far left)* there form a protostar and surrounding disk (*rear, center*), which develop into a solar system like our own (rear, right). The star eventually becomes a red giant (*front, right*) and then a white dwarf (*front, left*).

Sun's Age (millions of years)	Key Developments in Sun's Life
0	First contraction of matter from nebula into early Sun, or protostar. Early planets, or protoplanets, begin to form within swirling rings of solar nebula disk.
1	Hot core of protostar forms from contraction.
10	Protostar contraction ends. Nuclear fusion of hydrogen at core begins, and the Sun becomes a "main-sequence" star.
4,600	The Sun today. It has grown, and continues to grow, gradually brighter and larger, very slowly causing temperatures on Earth to rise.
12,000	Sun begins burning hydrogen in a shell around a helium core and starts getting brighter and larger, developing into a red giant. Its life as a main-sequence star is over.
12,250	Sun begins helium fusion in its core, while continuing to burn hydrogen in surrounding shell. Sun shrinks and becomes less bright.
12,350	With helium in core used up, Sun begins burning helium in surrounding shell and enters second red-giant phase. Its surface expands, eventually extending possibly as far as Earth's orbit.
12,365	Dying Sun begins giving off gas and dust that form a "planetary" nebula, leaving behind the hot burned-out core – a white dwarf star.
Unknown	White dwarf cools into a black dwarf, taking billions of years.

More Books about Our Planetary System

Beyond : Visions Of The Interplanetary Probes. Michael Benson (Abrams)
Exploring Our Solar System. Sally Ride and Tam E. O'Shaughnessy (Crown)
Our Solar System. Seymour Simon (Morrow)
The Solar System. Christopher Cooper (Raintree)
The Solar System. Robin Kerrod (Lerner)

DVDs

The Planets. (A & E Entertainment)
Voyage to the Outer Planets & Beyond. (Aae Films)

Web Sites

The Internet is a good place to get more information about our Solar System. The web sites listed here can help you learn about the most recent discoveries, as well as those made in the past.

NASA, Solar System Exploration. sse.jpl.nasa.gov/index.cfm
NASA, Solar System Simulator. space.jpl.nasa.gov/index.html
National Geographic, Virtual Solar System. www.nationalgeographic.com/solarsystem/
The Nine Planets. www.nineplanets.org/
Views of the Solar System. www.solarviews.com/eng/homepage.htm
Windows to the Universe.
www.windows.ucar.edu/tour/link=/our_solar_system/solar_system.html

Places to Visit

Here are some museums and planetariums where you can find a variety of exhibits about our Solar System.

**Adler Planetarium and
 Astronomy Museum**
1300 S. Lake Shore Drive
Chicago, IL 60605-2403

American Museum of Natural History
Rose Center for Earth and Space
Central Park West at 79th Street
New York, NY 10024

Montreal Planetarium
1000, rue Saint-Jacques Ouest
Montréal (Québec) H3C 1G7
Canada

Museum of Science, Boston
Science Park
Boston, MA 02114

National Air and Space Museum
Smithsonian Institution
6th and Independence Avenue SW
Washington, DC 20560

Scienceworks Museum
2 Booker Street
Spotswood, Melbourne, Victoria 3015
Australia

Glossary

asteroids: very small "planets." More than a million of them exist in our Solar system. Most of them orbit the Sun between Mars and Jupiter.

binary stars: stars that circle each other.

black hole: a massive object so tightly packed that not even light can escape the force of its gravity.

comet: object in the Solar System made of ice, rock, and dust. When its orbit brings it closer to the Sun, it develops a tail of gas and dust.

fusion: the collision and combination of atoms of one kind of element to produce another, in the process releasing energy. For example, the fusion of hydrogen atoms can produce helium.

galaxy: a large star system containing up to hundreds of billions of stars, along with gas and dust. Our own galaxy is called the Milky Way.

gas giants: Jupiter, Saturn, Uranus, and Neptune; the farthest planets from the Sun - not counting Pluto. They consist mostly of the gases hydrogen and helium, rather than rock and metal.

helium: a light, colorless gas.

hydrogen: a colorless, odorless gas that is the simplest and lightest of the elements.

Kuiper Belt: region of the Solar System that exends beyond the orbit of Neptune and contains numerous icy and rocky bodies, the biggest of which are larger than the biggest asteroids.

light-year: the distance traveled by light in one year; it is equal to about 5.88 trillion miles (9.46 trillion km).

meteor: a tiny asteroid or meteoroid that has entered Earth's atmosphere. Also, the bright streak of light made as the meteoroid enters or moves through the atmosphere.

meteorite: a meteoroid when it hits Earth.

meteoroid: a lump of rock or metal drifting through space. Meteoroids can be as big as little asteroids or as small as specks of dust.

NASA: the National Aeronautics and Space Administration - the government space agency of the United States.

natural satellites: another name for the moons that orbit planets.

nebula: a cloud of gas and dust in space.

Oort Cloud: a grouping of comets in the outermost reaches of the Solar System. It is named after the Dutch astronomer Jan Oort, who suggested its existence in 1950.

orbit: the path that one celestial object follows as it circles, or revolves around, another.

Pluto: the farthest and smallest planet in our Solar System. It is located in the Kuiper Belt; some astronomers do not regard it as a real planet.

proto-: the earliest or first form of something. The young Sun may thus be referred to as a "protostar" or "proto-Sun," and the early planets may be called "protoplanets."

rocky planets: Mercury, Venus, Earth, and Mars; the planets closest to the Sun. They all have rock and metal at their centers.

Solar System: the Sun with the planets and all the other bodies, such as asteroids and comets, that orbit it.

white dwarf: the small, dense-hot body that remains when a star like our Sun collapses.

Index

Born in 1920, Isaac Asimov came to the United States as a young boy from his native Russia. As a young man, he was a student of biochemistry. In time, he became one of the most productive writers the world has ever known. His books cover a spectrum of topics, including science, history, language theory, fantasy, and science fiction. His brilliant imagination gained him the respect and admiration of adults and children alike. Sadly, Isaac Asimov died shortly after the publication of the first edition of *Isaac Asimov's Library of the Universe.*

The publishers wish to thank the following for permission to reproduce copyright material: front cover, 3, 8, 9 (both), © David Hardy; 4 (both), 7 (both), 28, © Tom Miller; 5, National Optical Astronomy Observatories; 10-11, 16, 20, NASA/JPL; 12, © Lynette Cook 1988; 13, 15 (lower), 17, 18, 24, NASA; 14, © Lynette Cook 1987; 15 (upper), 19 (lower), NASA/JPL/Space Science Institute; 19 (upper), © Kurt Burmann 1987; 21, © David Tholen, Institute for Astronomy, University of Hawaii; 22, José R. Díaz, *Sky & Telescope* Magazine, © 1993 Sky Publishing Corp.; 23 (upper), © Julian Baum; 23 (lower), © Dennis Milon; 25 (upper), NASA/JPL-Caltech/R. Hurt (SSC-Caltech); 25 (lower), © George East; 26, C. Burrows and J. Krist (STScI), WFPC2 IDT Team, NASA, ESA; 27 (upper), NASA/JPL-Caltech); 27 (lower), © John Foster; 29, © Brian Sullivan 1988.